DEDICATION

Devin, Creed, Ellie –
I will never meet anyone more like me
than you three,
literally.

WHAT'S INSIDE

ACKNOWLEDGMENTS

If you can relate, I need an external motivator to finish a large creative project. The shove this time came courtesy of the year-long '52 Project", created and led by Sue Mitchell. It was strongly supported by the Riverside Art Museum, and underwritten by small donations from across the place I love and call home, Riverside, CA.
Thank you to my 140+ fel ow students; I consider you partners in this little art heist we pulled! I promise to remember the lessons each of you taught, and teach them to others.

9:00 @ Starbucks.
Boys, Do your chores ☺
-Gracias – Love, Dad

A typical note. - LB

Lost Ball

We tossed that old ball
With the loose stitches
And scuffed surface
Until you reared back
Hurled a high hard one
Just to see if you could do it.
A glancing blow off
My fingertips
Bounding into the tall growing-wild "landscape"
Beside our house.

Given all the conditions
It could not have rolled
More than a few feet into
That untouched terrain
Which parts where you tread
And closes in after
You move on.
The kind of place
For hiding if you went down on your knees.

We beat that plot
Side by side
First with laughter
Then a plow hand's precision
Until the pollen made me sneeze
And your socks filled with stickers.
The sun rolled far enough to

Declare that old ball lost
To rot or spring out again like a
Missile
Should we ever be foolish enough
To mow that side again.

When You Are Grown

You will know.
The world is better
Filled with easy answers.
Reason promises resolution
But delivers a horizon by design flawed.
When a round world circles
A round sun, you will
Never reach the place where
The sun sets.

Fortune then?
To be plucked up and plopped down
In the way back when?

When the land was flat
And done and still, its four corners
Known and held against the grid
By family, role, religion and economy,
Sure hands all.
None of that one hand clapping
Nonsense splayed out today.
Blood
Community
Church
State
Those are the hooks I would give
My own life to hang upon once again.

Your Face

more like hers than mine
but that's fine
When yelled at I see me p enty.
the shaking hands.
like leaves or rattlesnake
with red cheeks clenched teeth and dark eyes
So I stop with admonishments
turn over to warnings.
Don't be the me we've seen
be the me buried alive.
shout back.
swing fists.
when those muscles go unused
you die.

Do your chores, love dad

He Walks

Hands splayed before him
serving as guides, interpreters and advisors
along the lazy path
that cuts softly into the
earth with wildflowers playing at
the edges.
Tombstones loom at the horizon
looming tombstones wait for their
turn to possess those reaching hands.

Lighthouse

Looking out
over the sea of
young minds and whole limbs
I already mourn their deaths.
Their ignorance
About the years to
come pains me and I
rush sometimes
to clear paths and cover others.

Do your chores, love dad

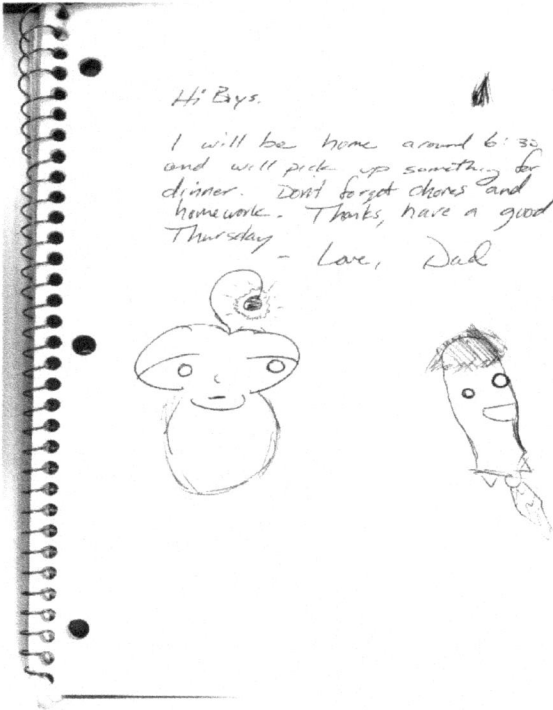

Hi Boys,
I will be home around 6:30 and will pick up something for
dinner. Don't forget chores and homework. Thanks, have a
good Thursday. – Love, Dad

*So many lines in the notebook were dedicated to food. The
drawings started as lines I would draw, then one of the boys,
or their friends, would make it into something. - LB*

Aches and Panes

He sees people mixed up
like a palette
under rain;
dogs are friends
needing many hugs and
help with their hair.

At Poppa and Mamaw's he counts
wind chimes and tickles
them when
breezes blow elsewhere.

He eyes gourmet foods
as something to mistrust
and cannot let chocolate melt
in his mouth.

A good day is when I am home.
For that, I am eternally grateful.

Path of Pebbles

What can you do with a stone?
Carry it
        Sit on it
              Roll it down a hill
                    Flatten a foe
                          Drop it

                          Wear it
                          down and make
                          a path of
                          pebbles.

binky

I found a four leaf clover
Which brings me lots of luck
Ensuring dreams of heroic acts
Which, beneath my pill nightly, I tuck.

The little green gift bereft of bloom
This happened token of fortune.

I'm grateful for its gifts
Before this my life was drudgery
A trial.
A bit of no fun.

With it around, I can
Sleep easy and rest in peace
Placed near my ear nestled like a contented bird
So it can whisper my destiny
To me.

I am singled out for special things
I am more equal than my peers
This little gift from nature
A raise from the burden
Of my fears.

Do your chores, love dad

Held

My childhood is always blank or selected stills
Because it was good.
McCourt and others are savants to theirs,
Each grimy crease in the bitter brick wall,
Named and cataloged and now.
Worked like a chewed spot on the inside of a soft cheek,
Or the callous on a dog's leg.

Metapresent and unresolved was fumbles the is.
So it cannot be forgotten.
It cannot be a memory in such a state.

But things can only be in one place at a time. Room for one and no more.
When the then is here it leaves a hole behind.
Black and longing, gravely situated.

Pulling us and everything associated with us like lemon taffy
Tart, sticky, old fashioned from old stuffing.
Working with sticky little hands, nails bitten to nubs
In defense against the hunger.
Knocking an arthritic *shave and a haircut*
From that cul-de-sac, the concave of a skull.

LARRY BURNS

Straight lines and nature

It takes but a little
To make a little man.
Imagine a small space
And the man and his parts
Appear larger.
Give him small things
And accomplishments too.
His hands, his mind
Will push the borders
Of his terrarium.
All his days until he
Believes he built the walls himself.

Do your chores, love dad

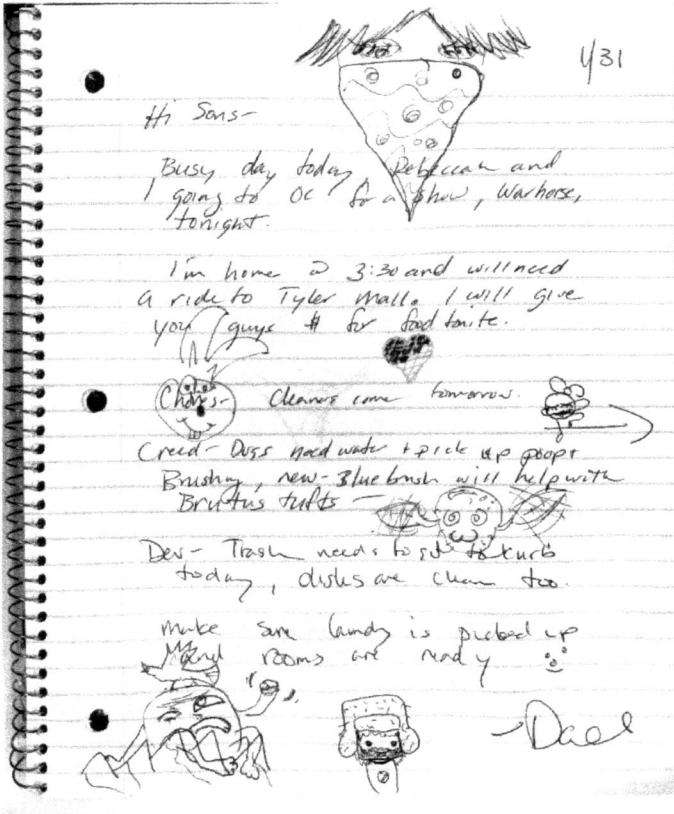

Hi Sons – 1/31
Busy day today, Rebeccah and I going to OC for a show, Warhorse, tonight.
I'm home @ 3:30 and will need a ride to Tyler Mall. I will give you guys $ for food tonite.
Cleaners come tomorrow.
Creed-Dogs need water & pick up poop & Brush, new Blue brush will help with Brutus tufts-
Dev- Trash needs to go to curb today, dishes are clean too.
make sure laundry is picked up and rooms are ready ☺

Uncle Felix's Photo Album

Is an eggshell colored
Shopping bag with
Reinforced handles and
"Neidsen-Forsen" in bold gold
Lettering along both broad sides.
"Another long gone department store"
He said with a smile when I asked.

I come to visit, reach blindly into the
Soup, pictures tattered, bent, variously sized
Cataloged by the last hand in the bag.
Each one holding a story to tell, Uncle Felix
Telling me about my family before I came along.
When everyone I love was young and free and
Standing near a photographer.
Often he would stop in the middle of the tale,
And like a magician pull another picture from
The bag, bringing it into the light like a surprised rabbit,
The story running through my grasp
In a new direction, with characters that
Were young and went old before I was even a
possibility.

Sometimes I would pocket one that caught my eye
And sometimes Uncle Felix would smile like he did
When he thought about Neidsen-Forsen and pretend
Not to notice.

Do your chores, love dad

The young boy sat

Pensive.
Laid out on the smooth mahogany table,
The Book.
Splayed out suggestively
To page 39, Chapter 2.
The characters introduced,
The plot just beginning
To hitch its skirt for
A peek at the world below.
That void to imprint upon
All beckoning and darkness.

A sinewy blotchy hair flecked arm
Reaches over his right
Shoulder near the place
Where his new hair cut itches.

A House is Pretty in the Dark

Beauty is not improved by sight.
Love is not improved by proximity.
In a long lived house
A person can walk with a
Hand on the wall, set low
So as to not knock a picture
Off the wall and scare everyone
With a shatter of glass in the loud dark hall.
Better to tour at night
Because memory can taint the
Present just so. The hall has
Days like when the boys
Were a little too rough and kicked
A hole in the drywall, right there.
And not it is a rough patch, not
Quite matching in color because
The paint is newer there now.

Do your chores, love dad

Everything was Fine

At eight I became everyone's friend.
Who does not love
a boy of all seasons?
Good test taker.
Good listener.
Plays well with all the others.
An S+ scholar.

At eighteen I became everyone's friend.
Quick on the line
But not too quick!
Already knew which side
buttered my bread.
It did not take a genius
to know I meant business.

At twenty eight, I became everyone's friend.
A dandelion in the academic garden.
A boy in a girl school,
A Canaanite who tunneled back into the Garden
with some right answers for the class,
but not too many.

At thirty eight, I became everyone's friend.
In the yard, the boys play while I work it,
giving a "Good Morning"
to my neighbors as I
rendered the weeds.
Then, in that easy chair,

bought in cash with a home
cooked meal in my belly,
I forgot myself and reflected:
Everyone did not love me.

Do your chores, love dad

Clean at Last
With the quiet settling
like fog from the ceiling
towards rugs so Persian
they are American.

I can keep a tidy place.

With them gone
no mud will traffic here
just the mysterious dead fly
on the odd sill.

No wants to be met
and every channel on
the finger-print-free TV
is mine all mine.

This house is a can of pop
left out
untouched
useless
going warm
and flat.

Sometimes the art seemed more fun to do, and better at conveying a message. What's this say? No clue.

Unmanly

How can a man not embrace his children? Love their future and test muscles to build it maintain it then die, so it may be theirs? Only a god would be so wise. Who are those imposters of men who reverse the equation? For them a child is a resource a trapping a receptacle a neat feat to be used and plowed.

Just Because we can always make more. We can always make more.

Papa

My Father carriers a small scar. A self-inflicted wound when, as a child in his Father's image, he pulled back a mighty claw-hammer to teach the new nail a neat magic trick only to find his world open wide in red stars that fell from the now unsmooth forehead. The wound, as you may have guessed, was not life-threatening. But it is the story that's stuck in my head now and always. It is the one I like to tell to anyone who will listen.

Scratch Marks

Quicklytheyscuttle
Through the green grass
Growing from good earth.

Their footprints will stay
But briefly in the bended
Blade but long after
They promote to other
Places and paths I will perceive
Them here, my view long
And back.

A sutra sodden prayer wheel
Spinning spinster yarns.

When Things Go to Pieces

The thing to remember about pieces
is that they go together
most nearly as nice as they
come apart.

Do not take it personally when
they do because
that is what pieces are here to do.

You are here to watch all this
and write it down when
the pen is handy or the
mood strikes you.

Household Tips for Men

Even if you tilt your head,
A crooked picture stays
Crooked.
You have to leave the room
And tuck the door into its frame
To put it straight.

A pot will fix a leaky roof
For about two days
Depending upon the temperament of the skies
And the size of the pot.

The best stain remover
On the market today
Is mahogany end table
You can ask for it by name
But plant stand will do if they're out.

And if a fool were
To wash a wool sweater in hot water
Just set it aside,
Next to the missing socks
Then buy her an early birthday present.

Sometimes I Lied to You + Sometimes I Did Not

Truth is, it's...it's....hell, I got nothin' son.
That's ok dad, I wasn't listening anyway.

Do your chores, love dad

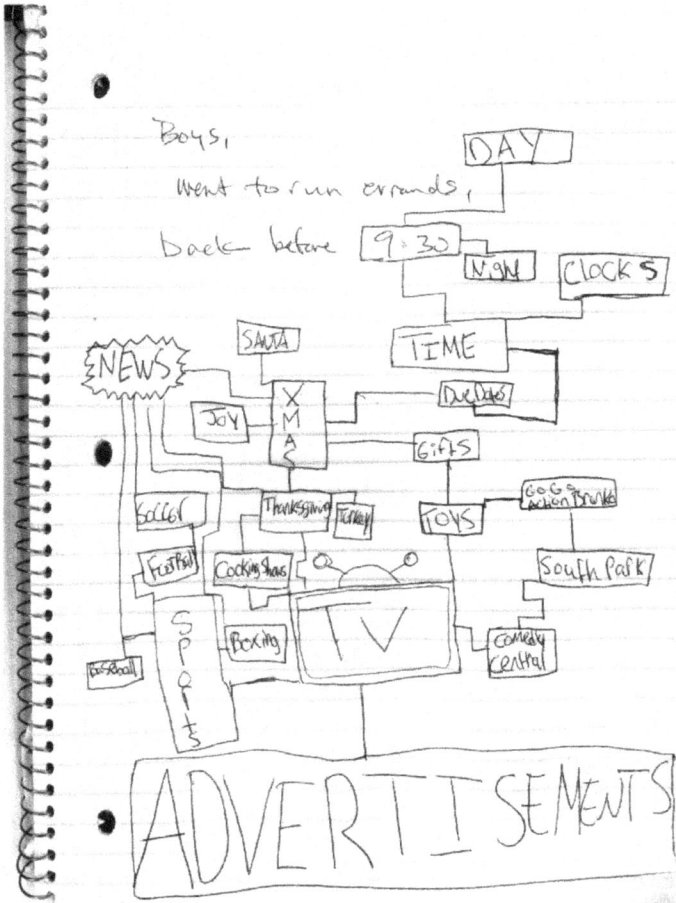

Boys, went to run errands, back before 9:30.

I like how the entire chart generates from a question of which version of 9:30 I will back before.

ABOUT THIS BOOK & THE 52 PROJECT

This is a companion piece to an art exhibit of the same
title. It appeared as part of a two month summer series
of mini-exhibitions at the Riverside Art Museum,
consisting of nearly three dozen "newish" artists. This is
my first book of poetry and my first creation to appear
in a museum.

This project captures one father's low-tech effort to
communicate with his sons. The plywood and copy
paper collage, as well as the poetry chapbook's
design, are influenced by the primary raw materials
used in this exhibit: spiral bound notebooks. Seven
notebooks of messages and doodles were copied, cut,
and reordered to illustrate how people make-up family
bonds and roles using complex communication
systems.

Fear was the catalyst. Fear I was losing my connection
to my children. Fear they would be harmed by my
divorce. Fear that an identity and worldview honed
over two decades of marriage was gone and I had no
idea how to fill that hole. So I started writing notes to
them. These were mostly reminders about chores,
dinner plans, and where I could be found. We added
doodles, then more detailed drawings and puns, as a
way to entertain each other. The project is proof that
the power to destroy and create anything worthwhile is
in our hands.

www.ingramcontent.com/pod-product-compliance
Lightning Source LLC
Chambersburg PA
CBHW060647030426
42337CB00018B/3495